· T R O P H I E S ·

# Decoding and Word Recognition Assessments

······································································

## Grade 1

**Harcourt**

Orlando   Austin   Chicago   New York   Toronto   London   San Diego

Visit *The Learning Site!*
**www.harcourtschool.com**

Printed in the United States of America

ISBN 0-15-337423-3

7  8  9  10   054   10  09  08  07  06  05

# Table of Contents

• • • • • • • • • • • • • • • • • • • • • • • • • • • • • • • • • • • • • • • • • • • • • • • •

**4**   **Purpose of the Assessments**

**4**   **Organization and Format of the Assessments**

    4   Sound-Letter Relationships

    5   Decodable Words

    5   High-Frequency Words

    5   Reading Sentences/Oral Reading

**6**   **Content of the Assessments**

**9**   **Administering the Assessments**

**10**   **Scoring and Interpreting the Assessments**

    10   Checkups 1 through 12

    11   Checkups 13 through 16

    11   Checkups 17 through 20

    12   Accuracy versus Fluency

**14**   **Tracking Progress**

**17**   **Checkups I through 20**
      **(including End-of-Book Checkups)**

# Purpose of the Assessments

These individual assessments are intended to carefully monitor children's acquisition of beginning decoding and word recognition skills taught in *Trophies Grade 1*. These assessments evaluate a child's knowledge of sound-letter relationships, ability to decode unfamiliar words, ability to identify high-frequency words at sight, and fluency in oral reading. The assessments build on the phonics and word recognition skills taught in *Trophies Kindergarten*.

The *Decoding and Word Recognition Assessments* are cumulative. They are designed to be administered after approximately every two to three instructional lessons and at the end of each book. They measure the sound-letter relationships, phonograms, and high-frequency words taught in those lessons as well as selected skills and strategies previously taught.

The intent of these supplemental assessments is to continuously monitor the learning and skill mastery of children who have been identified as "at risk learners." By frequently monitoring these children, adjustments can be made in instruction so they can maintain steady progress.

# Organization and Format of the Assessments

The *Decoding and Word Recognition Assessments* consist of a series of 15 Lesson Checkups plus 5 cumulative End-of-Book Checkups. Each one-page Checkup assesses the decoding and word recognition skills taught in the previous two to three lessons. In addition, the Checkups cumulatively assess skills and strategies taught in earlier lessons.

Four tasks, or subtests, are used on the Checkups.

## Sound-Letter Relationships

These items assess a child's ability to produce a spoken sound (phoneme) for a written letter or letter combination (grapheme). The teacher points to individual letters or letter combinations, and the child makes the sound associated with the letters. Both uppercase and lowercase letters are used.

**Example**

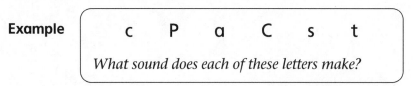

c   P   a   C   s   t

*What sound does each of these letters make?*

The assessment of sound-letter relationships progresses from individual letters to letter combinations (digraphs and blends), and eventually to decodable words and sentences.

This subtest is phased out after Checkup 12. Beginning with Checkup 13, sound-letter relationships are assessed in the context of decodable words and sentences.

### Decodable Words

This subtest assesses a child's ability to read decodable words containing phonic and structural elements that have been taught, such as consonants, phonograms, inflectional endings, and vowel patterns. The child pronounces the words independently.

Example
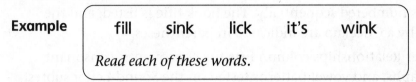

fill    sink    lick    it's    wink

*Read each of these words.*

### High-Frequency Words

This subtest assesses a child's ability to recognize the high-frequency words taught in the program.

Example
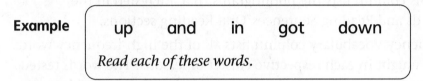

up    and    in    got    down

*Read each of these words.*

### Reading Sentences/Oral Reading

This subtest assesses a child's ability to apply his or her decoding skills in contextual situations. In the early Checkups, children are asked to read short, simple sentences comprised of a combination of decodable and high-frequency words. Later in the school year, the sentences increase in length and complexity. For example, structural analysis elements such as inflections and contractions are added to decodable words. Finally, beginning with Checkup 17, attention shifts from reading isolated sentences to reading short paragraphs with fluency.

Example

A ham will fit in the sack.
Lil wants the pink hat.
I'll help you pack now.

*Read these sentences aloud.*

# Content of the Assessments

The content of these assessments parallels the instructional content of the Grade 1 *Trophies* program.

The table on pages 7 and 8 summarizes the content of the *Decoding and Word Recognition Assessments*. The following guidelines will help you interpret the table.

- Each Checkup is numbered sequentially. The book title is listed, and the lessons covered by a Checkup are indicated in parentheses.

- The Sound-Letter Relationships column lists the consonants, consonant blends and digraphs, and vowel patterns tested on the Sound-Letter subtest of each Checkup. Beginning with Checkup 13, the sound-letter relationships are tested in the Decodable Words and Reading Sentences/Oral Reading sections.

- The Phonograms column lists the phonograms that are tested in the Decodable Words and Reading Sentences/Oral Reading sections.

- The High-Frequency Vocabulary column lists all of the high-frequency words that have been taught in each respective cluster of lessons. The words tested in the High-Frequency Words subtest are printed in boldface type. Many of the other high-frequency words (those not in boldface) are tested in the Reading Sentences/Oral Reading subtest in subsequent Checkups.

- The Structural Analysis column lists the structural elements (e.g., contractions, inflections) that are tested on each Checkup. These structural elements are assessed on the Decodable Words and Reading Sentences/Oral Reading subtests.

# Content of the Decoding and Word Recognition Assessments

| Checkup No. (Lessons) | Sound-Letter Relationships | Phonograms | High-Frequency Vocabulary | Structural Analysis |
|---|---|---|---|---|
| **Guess Who** | | | | |
| **1** (Lessons 1–2) | /a/*a*, /k/*c*, /p/*p*, /t/*t*, /s/*s* | –ap, –at | **down, got, up, and, in,** oh, yes | Inflection –s |
| **2** (Lessons 3–4) | /i/*i*, /l/*l*, /w/*w*, /f/*f*, /h/*h*; digraph /k/*ck* | –ill, –it, –ick, –ink | **make, they, walk,** help, now, **play, too,** want | Inflection –s; Contractions 's, 'll; |
| **3** (Lessons 5–6) | /o/*o*, /ô/*a* (all), /v/*v*, /ks/*x*, /m/*m*, /b/*b* | –all, –ill | don't, **of, so, buy,** that, **very, where** | Inflections –ed, –ing (no spelling change); Contraction n't |
| **4** (Lessons 1–6) **End-of-Book** | /t/*t*, /i/*i*, /a/*a*, /o/*o*; /ô/*a* (all); digraph /k/*ck* | –ink, –ick, –ill, –it, –all | **help, want, yes, don't, oh** | Inflections –s, –ed, –ing (no spelling change); Contractions 'll, 's, n't |
| **Catch a Dream** | | | | |
| **5** (Lessons 1–2) | /e/*e*; /d/*d*, /r/*r*; digraph /th/*th*; blends with *s* | –est, –ent | day, **every, her,** said, was, with, **could,** friends, **new,** put, she, **use** | Inflections –s, –ed, –ing (no spelling change) |
| **6** (Lessons 3–4) | /u/*u*; /j/*j*, /z/*z*, /k/*k*; blends with *r* | –ang, –ing | **gives,** he, **night,** out, people, says, when, your, eat, **from, gone, grows,** or, two | Inflection –s; Contraction 's; Possessive 's |
| **7** (Lessons 5–6) | /ôr/*or, ore*; /f/*f, ff*; digraph /sh/*sh*; blends with *r* and *s* | none | be, good, Mr., need, our, **right,** saw, time, try, **away, funny,** food, **hide,** how, many, some, **their** | Contraction 's; Possessive 's; Compound words |
| **8** (Lessons 1–6) **End-of-Book** | /u/*u*; /e/*e*; /ôr/*or, ore*; digraph /th/*th*; digraph /sh/*sh*; blends with *r* and *s* | –est, –ent, –ing, –ang | **friends, saw, good, people, how** | Inflections –s, –ed, –ing (no spelling change); Contraction 'll; Possessive 's; Compound words |
| **Here and There** | | | | |
| **9** (Lessons 1–2) | Digraph /ch/*ch, tch*; blends with *l*; /är/*ar*, /g/*g* | none | **air,** animals, around, **fly,** live, **soon, turns, city,** house, sometimes, take, there | Inflections –s, –ed, –ing (no spelling change); Contractions 's, 'll; Possessive 's |
| **10** (Lessons 3–4) | Digraphs /kw/*qu*, /hw/*wh*; /ûr/*er, ir, ur*; /n/*n* | none | about, books, by, **family, grew,** read, **work,** writing, find, follow, found, four, **full,** these, **way,** were | Inflections –s, –es, –ed, –ing (no spelling change); Contractions 've, 're; Compound words |
| **11** (Lessons 5–6) | /əl/–*le*; /ō/*ow, oa*; y/*y*; blends with *r* and *l* | none | **each,** great, other, place, school, talk, together, **door, kind, made,** who, **would** | Inflections –er, –est; –s, –ed, –ing (no spelling change) |
| **12** (Lessons 1–6) **End-of-Book** | /är/*ar*; /ûr/*er, ir, ur*; /ō/*ow, oa*; Digraphs /ch/*ch, tch*; /kw/*qu*; /hw/*wh* | none | **take, by, writing, about, other** | Inflections –er, –est; –s, –ed, –ing (no spelling change); Contraction 've; Possessive 's; Compound words |

| Checkup No. (Lessons) | Sound-Letter Relationships | Phonograms | High-Frequency Vocabulary | Structural Analysis |
|---|---|---|---|---|
| **Time Together** | | | | |
| **13** (Lessons 1–3) | /ē/*e, ee, ea;* /ā/ *a-e;* /ē/*y* | –ake, –ate | also, know, moved, **only**, room, **should**, those, **write, over,** town, **world,** different, old, water, years | Inflections –s; –ed, –ing (drop *e*); –es, –ed (change *y* to *i*); Contraction n't |
| **14** (Lessons 4–6) | /ī/*i-e;* /s/*c;* /ou/*ow, ou* | –ine, –ite, –ice, –ide, –own, –ound | because, **most,** picture, why, always, does, **even,** pretty, **say, sound, any,** took | Inflections –s, –ed (drop *e*); Contractions 's, 'll; Compound words |
| **15** (Lessons 7–8) | /ī/*y, ie;* /ō/*o-e* | none | **again,** blue, **high,** love, **opened, another, change** | Inflections –s, –ed –ing (no spelling change); –es (change *y* to *i*); –ed, –ing (drop *e*); Contraction n't |
| **16** (Lessons 1–8) **End-of-Book** | /ē/*e, ee, ea;* /ā/ *a-e;* /ē/*y* /ī/*y, ie;* /ō/*o-e* /ī/*i-e;* /s/*c;* /ou/*ow, ou* | –ake, –ate, –ine, –ite, –ice, –ide, –own, –ound | **always, does, also, years, know** | Inflections –er, –est; –s, –ed (no spelling change); –es, –ed (change *y* to *i*); –ed, –ing (drop *e*); Contractions 's, 'll, n't; Possessive 's; Compound words |
| **Gather Around** | | | | |
| **17** (Lessons 1–2) | /ī/*igh;* /ā/*ai, ay* | –ail, –ain | **nothing, thought, cold, sure** Review: **find** | Inflections –s, –ed (no spelling change; –ed, –ing (drop final *e*); –ed (change *y* to *i*); Possessive 's; Compound words |
| **18** (Lessons 3–5) | /ī/*i;* /ō/*o;* /j/*g, dge* | none | **both** Review: **how, together, took, were** | Inflections –s, –ing (no spelling change); –ed, –ing (double final consonant); –ed (drop *e*); Contractions 's, 've, 'd, 're, 'll; Possessive 's |
| **19** (Lessons 6–8) | /(y)o͞o/*u-e;* /ĕ/*ea;* /o͞o/*oo* | –oom, –oot | **boy, head, read** Review: **because, love** | Inflections –s, –ed (no spelling change); –ed (double final consonant); Contractions 's, 'll, 'd, 've, n't, 're; Compound words |
| **20** (Lessons 1–8) **End-of-Book** | /ī/*igh;* /ā/*ai, ay* /ī/*i;* /ō/*o;* /j/*g, dge* /(y)o͞o/*u-e;* /ĕ/*ea;* /o͞o/*oo* | –ail, –ain, –oom, –oot | **sure, both, nothing, cold, thought** | Inflections –s, –ed, –ing (no spelling change); –ed, –ing (double final consonant); –es; –ing (drop *e*) Contractions 's, 'd, n't, 're; Possessive 's |

# Administering the Assessments

The Checkups are informal assessments designed to inform instruction. They are not standardized tests. Therefore, feel free to create and modify the directions so that they are clear to the children.

The Checkups must be administered individually, since the items require oral responses. Two forms of each Checkup are provided in this manual—a form for the child to use, and a form for the teacher to use in recording responses. The student form is nonconsumable and can be reused for multiple administrations. A fresh copy of the teacher form should be created for each administration.

The Checkups are very short and focused. You should be able to administer a Checkup in about five minutes.

In general, follow these steps when administering the Checkups:

- Find a quiet setting in which to administer the Checkups. This will enhance the child's concentration and make it easier to hear the child's responses.

- Seat the child on one side of a table or desk with you on the other side so you can record your responses unobtrusively.

- Explain to the child that you want to find out how well he or she understands the new sounds and words the class has been learning. Tell the child that you will write down his or her responses to help you remember what is said. Record the child's name and the date at the top of the teacher's record form.

- Starting at the beginning of each Checkup, guide the child through each subtest. Give the child a reasonable time to respond. Record his or her responses on the teacher form.

- On the Sound-Letter Relationships subtest, if the child gives an alternative sound for a vowel, ask the child if there is another sound that letter makes. For example, if the targeted sound is the short "a" sound, and the child gives the long "a" sound, ask if there is another sound that letter makes.

- If the child becomes frustrated and unable to respond, stop the assessment.

- If you are administering the Oral Reading section, have a stopwatch or a clock with a second hand available to time the child's reading.

- Don't score and analyze the Checkup in front of the child. Wait to do that after the child has left.

# Scoring and Interpreting the Assessments

Scoring the assessments should be quick and straightforward. Each "item" is scored either correct or incorrect to obtain a child's raw score. The child's raw score is then compared to the expected score to determine whether to "Move Forward" or "Reteach."

## Checkups 1 through 12
(including End-of-Book Checkups for *Guess Who, Catch a Dream,* and *Here and There*)

Each of these Checkups consists of four sections or subtests. Follow these guidelines for scoring each subtest.

### Sound-Letter Relationships
- Treat each letter or letter combination as an item.
- Place a checkmark over a letter or letter combination for correct responses.
- Record a child's response phonetically for any incorrect responses.
- Record the number correct in the space provided in the margin.

### Decodable Words
- Treat each word as a separate item.
- Score the word correct if it is pronounced correctly.
- Score the word incorrect if it is pronounced incorrectly, and record the child's pronunciation phonetically.
- Record the number correct in the space provided in the margin.

### High-Frequency Words
- Treat each word as a separate item.
- Score the word correct if it is pronounced correctly.
- Score the word incorrect if it is pronounced incorrectly, and record the child's pronunciation phonetically.
- Record the number correct in the space provided.

### Reading Sentences
- Treat each word as a separate item.
- Record mispronunciations phonetically above the word.
- Circle any words that are skipped or omitted.
- Do not count repetitions and self-corrections as errors.
- Record the number of words read correctly in the space provided.

After scoring each of the four subtests and recording the scores in the margin, determine if the child meets the expected goal for each of the subtests. If the child meets the goal for 3 or 4 of the subtests, he or she is making adequate progress and should move forward in the program. If the child does not meet the expected goal for 2 or more of the subtests, he or she should receive additional practice and/or some reteaching of the decoding skills and high-frequency words tested before moving forward in the program.

© Harcourt

## Checkups 13 through 16
(including End-of-Book Checkup for *Time Together*)

Each of these Checkups consists of three sections or subtests. Follow these guidelines for scoring each subtest.

### Decodable Words
- Treat each word as a separate item.
- Score the word correct if it is pronounced correctly.
- Score the word incorrect if it is pronounced incorrectly, and record the child's pronunciation phonetically.
- Record the number correct in the space provided in the margin.

### High-Frequency Words
- Treat each word as a separate item.
- Score the word correct if it is pronounced correctly.
- Score the word incorrect if it is pronounced incorrectly, and record the child's pronunciation phonetically.
- Record the number correct in the space provided.

### Reading Sentences
- Treat each word as a separate item.
- Record mispronunciations phonetically above the word.
- Circle any words that are skipped or omitted.
- Do not count repetitions and self-corrections as errors.
- Record the number of words read correctly in the space provided.

## Checkups 17 through 20
(including End-of-Book Checkup for *Gather Around*)

Each of these Checkups consists of three sections or subtests. Follow these guidelines for scoring each subtest.

### Decodable Words
- Treat each word as a separate item.
- Score the word correct if it is pronounced correctly
- Score the word incorrect if it is pronounced incorrectly, and record the child's pronunciation phonetically.
- Record the number correct in the space provided.

### High-Frequency Words
- Treat each word as a separate item.
- Score the word correct if it is pronounced correctly.
- Score the word incorrect if it is pronounced incorrectly, and record the child's pronunciation phonetically.
- Record the number correct in the space provided.

### Oral Reading Accuracy and Fluency

- As the child reads the passage orally, record any mispronunciations and circle any omissions.
- Do not count repetitions and self-corrections as errors.
- Time the child as he or she reads. Make a single slash (/) in the text at the point the child reaches at 30 seconds.
- Treat each word as a separate item.
- Count the number of words read correctly and record that number in the space provided in the margin. Use the row numbers to help quickly count the number of words read correctly.
- Note whether the child meets the Accuracy Goals and Fluency Goals provided at the bottom of each passage.

## Accuracy versus Fluency

Research recognizes fluency as a strong indicator of efficient and proficient reading. A fluent reader reads orally with accuracy and expression, at a speech-like pace. Oral reading fluency is an assessment of accuracy and rate. It is expressed as the number of words read correctly per minute (WCPM).

> Total Number of Words Read in One Minute
> − Number of Reading Errors Made in One Minute
>
> Words Read Correctly per Minute (WCPM)

It is important to strive for a balance between accuracy and fluency. Children need to develop a degree of accuracy in decoding and word recognition *before* they are encouraged to increase reading rate and fluency. The following flowchart captures the relationship between accuracy and fluency. It shows the questions a teacher should ask in interpreting a child's performance and the instructional implications that result from those questions.

# Interpreting Performance on the Oral Reading Fluency Tasks

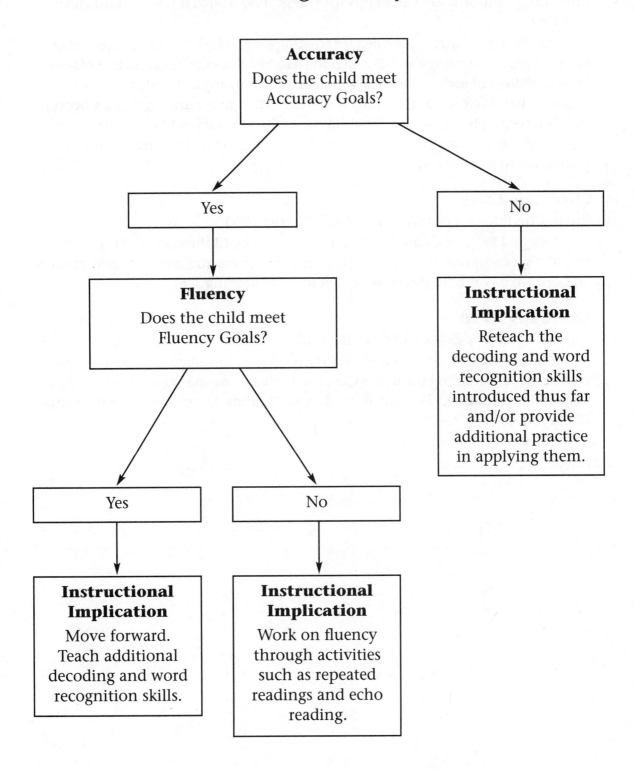

**Accuracy**
Does the child meet Accuracy Goals?

Yes

No

**Fluency**
Does the child meet Fluency Goals?

**Instructional Implication**
Reteach the decoding and word recognition skills introduced thus far and/or provide additional practice in applying them.

Yes

No

**Instructional Implication**
Move forward. Teach additional decoding and word recognition skills.

**Instructional Implication**
Work on fluency through activities such as repeated readings and echo reading.

# Tracking Progress

Three Progress Charts are included in this Manual to help teachers track a child's progress throughout the school year.

## Checkups 1 through 12
(including End-of-Book Checkups for *Guess Who, Catch a Dream,* and *Here and There*)

One Progress Chart is provided for Checkups 1 through 12. Space is provided on this form for marking the following: the date the Checkup is given, and mastery or non-mastery of each subtest—Sound-Letter Relationships, Decodable Words, High-Frequency Words, and Reading Sentences. After giving and scoring a Checkup, simply record a plus sign (+) if the child meets the goal for a subtest, and a minus sign (−) if the child does not meet the goal. Space is provided for any comments a teacher might want to add.

## Checkups 13–16
(including End-of-Book Checkup for *Time Together*)

A second Progress Chart is provided for Checkups 13 through 16. This form provides space for recording the date a Checkup is given, and master or non-mastery on Decodable Words, High-Frequency Words, and Reading Sentences.

## Checkups 17–20
(including End-of-Book Checkup for *Gather Around*)

A third Progress Chart is provided for Checkups 17 through 20. This form provides space for recording the date a Checkup is given, and master or non-mastery on Decodable Words, High-Frequency Words, Oral Reading Accuracy, and Oral Reading Fluency.

Name _____

Progress Chart
Checkups 1–12

Teacher _____

KEY:  + = Met goal        − = Did not meet goal

| Checkup Number | Date Given | Sound-Letter Relationships | Decodable Words | High-Frequency Words | Reading Sentences | Action Taken | | Comments |
|---|---|---|---|---|---|---|---|---|
| | | | | | | Move Forward | Reteach | |
| 1 | | | | | | | | |
| 2 | | | | | | | | |
| 3 | | | | | | | | |
| *4 | | | | | | | | |
| 5 | | | | | | | | |
| 6 | | | | | | | | |
| 7 | | | | | | | | |
| *8 | | | | | | | | |
| 9 | | | | | | | | |
| 10 | | | | | | | | |
| 11 | | | | | | | | |
| *12 | | | | | | | | |

* End-of-Book Checkup

Decoding and Word Recognition Assessments   15

# Progress Chart
## Checkups 13–16

Name _____  Teacher _____

KEY:  + = Met goal    − = Did not meet goal

| Checkup Number | Date Given | Decodable Words | High-Frequency Words | Reading Sentences | Action Taken | | Comments |
|---|---|---|---|---|---|---|---|
| | | | | | Move Forward | Reteach | |
| 13 | | | | | | | |
| 14 | | | | | | | |
| 15 | | | | | | | |
| *16 | | | | | | | |

# Progress Chart
## Checkups 17–20

| Checkup Number | Date Given | Decodable Words | High-Frequency Words | Oral Reading | | Action Taken | | Comments |
|---|---|---|---|---|---|---|---|---|
| | | | | Accuracy | Fluency | Move Forward | Reteach | |
| 17 | | | | | | | | |
| 18 | | | | | | | | |
| 19 | | | | | | | | |
| *20 | | | | | | | | |

* End-of-Book Checkup

Name _____ Date _____

# Checkup 1: (*Guess Who*, Lessons 1–2)

Sound-Letter Relationships          Goal: 6/6   Score ____/6

| | | | | | | |
|---|---|---|---|---|---|---|
| c | P | a | C | s | t |

Decodable Words          Goal: 3/3   Score ____/3

| | | |
|---|---|---|
| sat | tap | cats |

High-Frequency Words          Goal: 4/5   Score ____/5

| | | | | |
|---|---|---|---|---|
| up | and | in | got | down |

Reading Sentences          Goal: 8/9   Score ____/9

I can see you.
Yes, Pat likes the cap.

☐ **Move Forward:** The child meets the goals for at least 3 of the 4 subtests.

☐ **Reteach:** The child does not meet the goals for 2 or more of the subtests. Provide additional practice and retest.

c    P    a    C    s    t

sat      tap      cats

up    and    in    got    down

I can see you.

Yes, Pat likes the cap.

Name _____ Date _____

# Checkup 2: (*Guess Who*, Lessons 3–4)

Sound-Letter Relationships                                    Goal: 5/6    Score ____/6

| L | w | i | f | H | ck |
|---|---|---|---|---|----|

Decodable Words                                               Goal: 4/5    Score ____/5

| fill | sink | lick | it's | wink |
|------|------|------|------|------|

High-Frequency Words                                          Goal: 4/5    Score ____/5

| too | play | make | they | walk |
|-----|------|------|------|------|

Reading Sentences                                             Goal: 15/17   Score ____/17

A ham will fit in the sack.

Lil wants the pink hat.

I'll help you pack now.

☐ **Move Forward:** The child meets the goals for at least 3 of the 4 subtests.

☐ **Reteach:** The child does not meet the goals for 2 or more of the subtests. Provide additional practice and retest.

| v | x | B | o | all | M |
|---|---|---|---|-----|---|

| box | vat | mill | dock | falling |
|-----|-----|------|------|---------|

| of | very | so | buy | where |
|----|------|----|-----|-------|

Look at that big fox!

Don't you want to buy a ball?

Van walked up and down the hall.

## Checkup 4: End-of-Book (*Guess Who*, Lessons 1–6)

Sound-Letter Relationships                                    Goal: 5/6   Score ____/6

| t | i | ck | a | o | all |
|---|---|----|---|---|-----|

Decodable Words                                              Goal: 4/5   Score ____/5

| linking | Mick | billed | hit | walls |
|---------|------|--------|-----|-------|

High-Frequency Words                                         Goal: 4/5   Score ____/5

| help | want | yes | don't | oh |
|------|------|-----|-------|-----|

Reading Sentences                                            Goal: 22/24   Score ____/24

We'll pick up all the tacks now.

Didn't you fill that box to the very top?

They are playing where it's not too hot.

☐ **Move Forward:** The child meets the goals for at least 3 of the 4 subtests.

☐ **Reteach:** The child does not meet the goals for 2 or more of the subtests. Provide additional practice and retest.

Checkup 4

t    i    ck    a    o    all

linking    Mick    billed    hit    walls

help    want    yes    don't    oh

We'll pick up all the tacks now.

Didn't you fill that box to the very top?

They are playing where it's not too hot.

Name _____ Date _____

## Checkup 5: (*Catch a Dream*, Lessons 1–2)

Sound-Letter Relationships            Goal: 5/6   Score ____/6

| d | r | th | sp | st | e |
|---|---|----|----|----|---|

Decodable Words            Goal: 4/5   Score ____/5

| dent | thick | rest | spilled | stinks |
|------|-------|------|---------|--------|

High-Frequency Words            Goal: 4/5   Score ____/5

| use | every | new | her | could |
|-----|-------|-----|-----|-------|

Reading Sentences            Goal: 19/21   Score ____/21

Was Dad calling me?
I spent all day with my friends.
She said you could put the lamp
on that desk.

☐ **Move Forward:** The child meets the goals for at least 3 of the 4 subtests.

☐ **Reteach:** The child does not meet the goals for 2 or more of the subtests. Provide additional practice and retest.

d     r     th     sp     st     e

dent     thick     rest     spilled     stinks

use     every     new     her     could

Was Dad calling me?

I spent all day with my friends.

She said you could put the lamp
on that desk.

Name _____ Date _____

## Checkup 6: (*Catch a Dream*, Lessons 3–4)

Sound-Letter Relationships          Goal: 5/6 correct   Score ____/6

| j | u | z | k | br | dr |
|---|---|---|---|----|----|

Decodable Words          Goal: 4/5   Score ____/5

| bring | zip | sang | drink | Nick's |
|-------|-----|------|-------|--------|

High-Frequency Words          Goal: 4/5   Score ____/5

| from | gone | night | grows | gives |
|------|------|-------|-------|-------|

Reading Sentences          Goal: 27/30   Score ____/30

Two people got on the bus.

Buzz says that he plays the drums well.

Let's just hang your dress on that rack.

My pups make a mess when they eat.

☐ **Move Forward:** The child meets the goals for at least 3 of the 4 subtests.

☐ **Reteach:** The child does not meet the goals for 2 or more of the subtests. Provide additional practice and retest.

Checkup 6

| | | | | | |
|---|---|---|---|---|---|
| j | u | z | k | br | dr |

bring     zip     sang     drink     Nick's

from     gone     night     grows     gives

Two people got on the bus.

Buzz says that he plays the drums well.

Let's just hang your dress on that rack.

My pups make a mess when they eat.

Name _____ Date _____

## Checkup 7: (*Catch a Dream*, Lessons 5–6)

Sound-Letter Relationships                                        Goal: 5/6   Score _____/6

| or | sh | ff | fr | tr | sn |

Decodable Words                                                  Goal: 4/5   Score _____/5

| fork | snore | frog | stuff | trust |

High-Frequency Words                                            Goal: 4/5   Score _____/5

| right | funny | hide | their | away |

Reading Sentences                                              Goal: 29/32   Score _____/32

I did my best when we played kickball.

"We need some more popcorn," said Norm.

Mom will buy fresh corn and crab at
the store.

It's time for Mr. York's short nap.

☐ **Move Forward:** The child meets the goals for at least 3 of the 4 subtests.

☐ **Reteach:** The child does not meet the goals for 2 or more of the subtests. Provide additional practice and retest.

| or | sh | ff | fr | tr | sn |
|----|----|----|----|----|----|

| fork | snore | frog | stuff | trust |
|------|-------|------|-------|-------|

| right | funny | hide | their | away |
|-------|-------|------|-------|------|

I did my best when we played kickball.

"We need some more popcorn," said Norm.

Mom will buy fresh corn and crab at
the store.

It's time for Mr. York's short nap.

Name _____ Date _____

## Checkup 8: End-of-Book (*Catch a Dream*, Lessons 1–6)

Sound-Letter Relationships                    Goal: 5/6   Score ____/6

| u | sh | sm | th | e | or |

Decodable Words                               Goal: 4/5   Score ____/5

| tested | renting | swing | rang | thorns |

High-Frequency Words                          Goal: 4/5   Score ____/5

| friends | saw | good | people | how |

Reading Sentences                             Goal: 31/35   Score ____/35

Sometimes my pup brings me small sticks.
Kent's dad, Mr. King, will be trying to
win a truck or cash.
Many cats rest all day. Then they'll dash
out at night to hunt for food.

☐ **Move Forward:** The child meets the goals for at least 3 of the 4 subtests.

☐ **Reteach:** The child does not meet the goals for 2 or more of the subtests. Provide additional practice and retest.

Checkup 8

| u | sh | sm | th | e | or |

| tested | renting | swing | rang | thorns |

| friends | saw | good | people | how |

Sometimes my pup brings me small sticks.

Kent's dad, Mr. King, will be trying to win a truck or cash.

Many cats rest all day. Then they'll dash out at night to hunt for food.

## Checkup 9: (*Here and There*, Lessons 1–2)

Sound-Letter Relationships                     Goal: 5/6   Score ____/6

| ch | bl | ar | cl | fl | g |
|----|----|----|----|----|---|

Decodable Words                                 Goal: 4/5   Score ____/5

| black | itch | starch | clutch | flashed |
|-------|------|--------|--------|---------|

High-Frequency Words                            Goal: 4/5   Score ____/5

| air | city | fly | turns | soon |
|-----|------|-----|-------|------|

Reading Sentences                               Goal: 28/31   Score ____/31

How many animals live around there?

Art saw Chad pitching balls at Mitch's house.

Barb said, "Try this sandwich. It's good!"

We'll buy plums for our lunch when we go out.

□ **Move Forward:** The child meets the goals for at least 3 of the 4 subtests.

□ **Reteach:** The child does not meet the goals for 2 or more of the subtests. Provide additional practice and retest.

Checkup 9

| ch | bl | ar | cl | fl | g |

| black | itch | starch | clutch | flashed |

| air | city | fly | turns | soon |

How many animals live around there?

Art saw Chad pitching balls at Mitch's house.

Barb said, "Try this sandwich. It's good!"

We'll buy plums for our lunch when we go out.

© Harcourt

Name _____ Date _____

# Checkup 10: (*Here and There*, Lessons 3–4)

Sound-Letter Relationships                     Goal: 5/6   Score ____/6

| wh | ir | qu | ur | n | er |
|----|----|----|----|----|----|

Decodable Words                                Goal: 4/5   Score ____/5

| squirted | quart | burns | perches | which |
|----------|-------|-------|---------|-------|

High-Frequency Words                           Goal: 4/5   Score ____/5

| work | family | grew | way | full |
|------|--------|------|-----|------|

Reading Sentences                              Goal: 35/39   Score ____/39

Were these foods left out all night?
Sometimes Mr. Mills reads books to us
about animals.
Quinn is writing cards to thank her friends
for their birthday gifts.
We're following the chirping. We've found
four birds in their nest!

☐ **Move Forward:** The child meets the goals for at least 3 of the 4 subtests.

☐ **Reteach:** The child does not meet the goals for 2 or more of the subtests. Provide additional practice and retest.

| wh | ir | qu | ur | n | er |
|----|----|----|----|---|----|

| squirted | quart | burns | perches | which |
|----------|-------|-------|---------|-------|

| work | family | grew | way | full |
|------|--------|------|-----|------|

Were these foods left out all night?

Sometimes Mr. Mills reads books to us about animals.

Quinn is writing cards to thank her friends for their birthday gifts.

We're following the chirping. We've found four birds in their nest!

## Checkup 11: (*Here and There*, Lessons 5–6)

Sound-Letter Relationships                                    Goal: 5/6   Score ____/6

| ow | l | oa | gr | sl | y |

Decodable Words                                              Goal: 4/5   Score ____/5

| crows | griddle | coat | yell | slowest |

High-Frequency Words                                         Goal: 4/5   Score ____/5

| door | would | made | each | kind |

Reading Sentences                                           Goal: 35/39   Score ____/39

Tell a funny riddle to make us giggle.

The two girls like talking to each other and walking to school together.

Bert followed the road and found a great place to hide.

Who mowed the grass lower this time?

☐ **Move Forward:** The child meets the goals for at least 3 of the 4 subtests.

☐ **Reteach:** The child does not meet the goals for 2 or more of the subtests. Provide additional practice and retest.

| ow | l | oa | gr | sl | y |
|----|---|----|----|----|----|

| crows | griddle | coat | yell | slowest |
|-------|---------|------|------|---------|

| door | would | made | each | kind |
|------|-------|------|------|------|

Tell a funny riddle to make us giggle.

The two girls like talking to each other and walking to school together.

Bert followed the road and found a great place to hide.

Who mowed the grass lower this time?

© Harcourt

## Checkup 12: End-of-Book (*Here and There*, Lessons 1–6)

Sound-Letter Relationships                    Goal: 5/6   Score ____/6

| ch | qu | wh | ar | ir | oa |
|---|---|---|---|---|---|

Decodable Words                    Goal: 4/5   Score ____/5

| pickles | quarters | whacking | thirst | warmer |
|---|---|---|---|---|

High-Frequency Words                    Goal: 4/5   Score ____/5

| take | by | writing | about | other |
|---|---|---|---|---|

Reading Sentences                    Goal: 37/41   Score ____/41

Jill's mom stitched a patch on her torn coat.
Which store around there sells whistles?
The fastest car made a quick start. Then it
slowed and parked by the curb.
I've found someone who can make animals
out of blown glass!

☐ **Move Forward:** The child meets the goals for at least 3 of the 4 subtests.

☐ **Reteach:** The child does not meet the goals for 2 or more of the subtests. Provide additional practice and retest.

ch     qu     wh     ar     ir     oa

pickles     quarters     whacking     thirst     warmer

take     by     writing     about     other

Jill's mom stitched a patch on her torn coat.

Which store around there sells whistles?

The fastest car made a quick start. Then it slowed and parked by the curb.

I've found someone who can make animals out of blown glass!

Name _____ Date _____

# Checkup 13: (*Time Together*, Lessons 1–3)

Decodable Words                                            Goal: 4/5   Score ____/5

| teach | makes | hurry | creek | plate |

High-Frequency Words                                      Goal: 4/5   Score ____/5

| only | should | write | over | world |

Reading Sentences                                          Goal: 41/45   Score ____/45

Who carried water to those thirsty people?
Our family saved pennies for years to buy
our dream house.
Aren't Jake and Andy going skating later at
the lake?
The sleepy kitten moved from room to
room. It was looking around for a different
resting place.

☐ **Move Forward:** The child meets the goals for at least 3 of the 4 subtests.

☐ **Reteach:** The child does not meet the goals for 2 or more of the subtests. Provide additional practice and retest.

Checkup 13

teach    makes    hurry    creek    plate

only    should    write    over    world

Who carried water to those thirsty people?

Our family saved pennies for years to buy our dream house.

Aren't Jake and Andy going skating later at the lake?

The sleepy kitten moved from room to room. It was looking around for a different resting place.

## Checkup 14: (*Time Together*, Lessons 4–6)

Decodable Words                                           Goal: 4/5   Score ____/5

> vines     quite     crown     glided     price

High-Frequency Words                                      Goal: 4/5   Score ____/5

> any     even     sound     most     say

Reading Sentences                                         Goal: 31/35   Score ___/35

> Why does that clown always say silly things?
>
> Let's race our bikes around the block. Then we'll ride downtown for ice cream.
>
> The old man took the pictures outside because it was a pretty day.

☐ **Move Forward:** The child meets the goals for at least 3 of the 4 subtests.

☐ **Reteach:** The child does not meet the goals for 2 or more of the subtests. Provide additional practice and retest.

vines     quite     crown     glided     price

any     even     sound     most     say

Why does that clown always say silly things?

Let's race our bikes around the block. Then we'll ride downtown for ice cream.

The old man took the pictures outside because it was a pretty day.

## Checkup 15: (*Time Together*, Lessons 7–8)

Decodable Words                                    Goal: 4/5   Score ____/5

| stone | cry | lies | closed | frying |

High-Frequency Words                               Goal: 4/5   Score ____/5

| again | high | another | opened | change |

Reading Sentences                                  Goal: 37/41   Score ____/41

"Don't you just love puppies?" Joan asked.

Nine kites were dancing high in the blue sky.

Tony changed into another shirt and tie while his wet shirt was drying.

Jane is writing a note to thank her teacher for her help.

☐ ***Move Forward:*** The child meets the goals for at least 3 of the 4 subtests.

☐ ***Reteach:*** The child does not meet the goals for 2 or more of the subtests. Provide additional practice and retest.

stone     cry     lies     closed     frying

again     high     another     opened     change

"Don't you just love puppies?" Joan asked.

Nine kites were dancing high in the blue sky.

Tony changed into another shirt and tie while his wet shirt was drying.

Jane is writing a note to thank her teacher for her help.

© Harcourt

Name _____ Date _____

## Checkup 16: End-of-Book (*Time Together*, Lessons 1–8)

Decodable Words                                            Goal: 4/5    Score ____/5

| while | shaved | ounces | deepest | throne |

High-Frequency Words                                       Goal: 4/5    Score ____/5

| also | does | years | know | always |

Reading Sentences                                          Goal: 47/52    Score ____/52

I'll take a slice of Betsy's fine cherry pie, please.

He's traced a circle, but it doesn't look quite as round as it should.

We worried that the band would sound too loud if we moved closer.

Nate, close the window now. Flies will not keep coming inside if it is down.

☐ **Move Forward:** The child meets the goals for at least 3 of the 4 subtests.

☐ **Reteach:** The child does not meet the goals for 2 or more of the subtests. Provide additional practice and retest.

Checkup 16

while    shaved    ounces    deepest    throne

also    does    years    know    always

I'll take a slice of Betsy's fine cherry pie, please.

He's traced a circle, but it doesn't look quite as round as it should.

We worried that the band would sound too loud if we moved closer.

Nate, close the window now. Flies will not keep coming inside if it is down.

## Checkup 17: (*Gather Around*, Lessons 1–2)

Decodable Words                                      Goal: 4/5   Score ____/5

| snail | plain | trays | tight | sway |

High-Frequency Words                                 Goal: 4/5   Score ____/5

| sure | nothing | thought | cold | find |

Oral Reading    Have the child read the title and the entire passage. Start timing when the child begins reading. Make a single slash in the text (/) at 30 seconds.

| | |
|---|---|
| Jay's Room | 2 |
| In May, Jay's family moved to a new house. | 11 |
| Dad painted Jay's room with bright yellow paint. | 19 |
| When the paint dried, they hung pictures high on | 28 |
| the walls. | 30 |
| One picture shows a big red train racing down | 39 |
| some railroad tracks. | 42 |
| Another picture shows a small sailboat gliding on | 50 |
| blue water. | 52 |
| Very soon, Jay was happy in his new home. | 61 |

**Accuracy**          Goal: 55/61   Score ____/61

**Calculate Fluency**    Words Read Correctly in 30 Seconds        _____

                                                                    x 2

                        Words Read Correctly Per Minute (WCPM)    _____

**Fluency**    Goal: 30–50 wcpm   Score: ____wcpm

snail    plain    trays    tight    sway

sure    nothing    thought    cold    find

### Jay's Room

In May, Jay's family moved to a new house.

Dad painted Jay's room with bright yellow paint.

When the paint dried, they hung pictures high on the walls.

One picture shows a big red train racing down some railroad tracks.

Another picture shows a small sailboat gliding on blue water.

Very soon, Jay was happy in his new home.

## Checkup 18: (*Gather Around*, Lessons 3–5)

Decodable Words                                        Goal: 4/5   Score ____/5

| mold | hedge | grind | gentle | slipped |
|------|-------|-------|--------|---------|

High-Frequency Words                                   Goal: 4/5   Score ____/5

| both | how | together | took | were |
|------|-----|----------|------|------|

**Oral Reading**   Have children read the title and the entire passage. Start timing at the first word of the first line. Make a single slash in the text (/) at 30 seconds.

| | |
|---|---|
| Class Play | 2 |
| Miss Gold's class is putting on a play. They've | 11 |
| practiced for weeks. Some children have lines | 18 |
| to say out loud. Others will help out behind the | 28 |
| big stage. | 30 |
| The play is about different kinds of animals. | 38 |
| Albert, Ginger, Rob, and Kim will be talking | 46 |
| animals. They'll tell what it's like to be a beaver, | 56 |
| a gull, a fish, or a skunk. | 63 |
| "We'd be happy for you to see our play," Kim | 73 |
| told her friends. "You're sure to like it. You'll be | 83 |
| clapping when it's over!" | 87 |

**Accuracy**          Goal: 78/87   Score ____/87

**Calculate Fluency**   Words Read Correctly in 30 Seconds        _____
                                                                        x 2

Words Read Correctly Per Minute (WCPM)        _____

**Fluency**   Goal: 30–50 wcpm   Score: ____wcpm

mold     hedge     grind     gentle     slipped

both     how     together     took     were

## Class Play

Miss Gold's class is putting on a play. They've practiced for weeks. Some children have lines to say out loud. Others will help out behind the big stage.

The play is about different kinds of animals. Albert, Ginger, Rob, and Kim will be talking animals. They'll tell what it's like to be a beaver, a gull, a fish, or a skunk.

"We'd be happy for you to see our play," Kim told her friends. "You're sure to like it. You'll be clapping when it's over!"

## Checkup 19: (*Gather Around*, Lessons 6–8)

Decodable Words                                    Goal: 4/5   Score ____/5

| prunes | thread | mule | scooter | broom |

High-Frequency Words                               Goal: 4/5   Score ____/5

| head | because | boy | love | read |

Oral Reading   Have children read the title and the entire passage. Start timing at the first word of the first line. Make a single slash in the text (/) at 30 seconds.

|                                                          |     |
|----------------------------------------------------------|-----|
| A Fur Cap                                                | 3   |
| After breakfast, Gramps showed Luke an old               | 10  |
| raccoon cap. Gramps wore the cap when he was             | 19  |
| a little boy.                                            | 22  |
| Later, Gramps and Luke were ready to check on            | 31  |
| their garden. They found the garden all messed           | 39  |
| up! There were feathers on the ground. Birds             | 47  |
| had dug up the seeds they'd planted!                     | 54  |
| "We've got to frighten the birds away so they            | 63  |
| won't use our seeds for their food," Gramps said.        | 72  |
| Luke yelled, "I know! Let's put the fur cap in           | 82  |
| the garden. They'll think it's a cat, so they'll         | 91  |
| stay away!"                                              | 93  |
| Gramps grinned and said, "You're smart, Luke!"           | 100 |

**Accuracy**       Goal: 90/100   Score ___/100

**Calculate Fluency**    Words Read Correctly in 30 Seconds    _____
                                                               x 2

                         Words Read Correctly Per Minute (WCPM)  _____
**Fluency**              Goal: 30–50 wcpm   Score: ____wcpm

prunes    thread    mule    scooter    broom

head    because    boy    love    read

## A Fur Cap

After breakfast, Gramps showed Luke an old raccoon cap. Gramps wore the cap when he was a little boy.

Later, Gramps and Luke were ready to check on their garden. They found the garden all messed up! There were feathers on the ground. Birds had dug up the seeds they'd planted!

"We've got to frighten the birds away so they won't use our seeds for their food," Gramps said.

Luke yelled, "I know! Let's put the fur cap in the garden. They'll think it's a cat, so they'll stay away!"

Gramps grinned and said, "You're smart, Luke!"

## Checkup 20: End-of-Book (*Gather Around*, Lessons 1-8)

Decodable Words                                         Goal: 4/5   Score ____/5

| flight   boots   spreading   badges   mailed |
|---|

High-Frequency Words                                    Goal: 4/5   Score ____/5

| sure       both       nothing       cold       thought |
|---|

**Oral Reading**   Have children read the title and the entire passage. Start timing at the first word of the first line. Make a single slash in the text (/) at 30 seconds.

| A New Baby | 3 |
|---|---|
| Mrs. Wilder was having a baby boy! Kay was | 12 |
| not happy. Now she was the only child. She | 21 |
| wasn't sure that should change. | 26 |
| One night Mom stepped into Kay's room. | 33 |
| "We're afraid you aren't happy about the baby," | 41 |
| Mom said. "Can't you think of some good things | 50 |
| about him?" | 52 |
| Kay thought. "I suppose I'd always have | 59 |
| someone to play with. It might be fun to teach | 69 |
| him things when he's older. Maybe on rainy days | 78 |
| we could sail boats in puddles. Maybe he'd even | 87 |
| be cute when he's little." | 92 |
| "That's my girl!" said Mom, hugging Kay tightly. | 100 |

**Accuracy**        Goal: 90/100   Score ___/100

**Calculate Fluency**   Words Read Correctly in 30 Seconds        _____
                                                                        x 2

Words Read Correctly Per Minute (WCPM)        _____

**Fluency**   Goal: 30–50 wcpm   Score: ____wcpm

flight    boots    spreading    badges    mailed

sure    both    nothing    cold    thought

## A New Baby

Mrs. Wilder was having a baby boy! Kay was not happy. Now she was the only child. She wasn't sure that should change.

One night Mom stepped into Kay's room. "We're afraid you aren't happy about the baby," Mom said. "Can't you think of some good things about him?"

Kay thought. "I suppose I'd always have someone to play with. It might be fun to teach him things when he's older. Maybe on rainy days we could sail boats in puddles. Maybe he'd even be cute when he's little."

"That's my girl!" said Mom, hugging Kay tightly.

© Harcourt